IRISH WIT

QUIPS AND QUOTES

Tom Hay

summersdale

IRISH WIT

First published in 2009
New edition published in 2012
This edition copyright © Summersdale Publishers Ltd, 2012

Summersdale Publishers Ltd
46 West Street
Chichester
West Sussex
PO19 1RP
UK

www.summersdale.com

Printed and bound in China

ISBN: 978-1-84953-333-1

Substantial discounts on bulk quantities of Summersdale books are available to corporations, professional associations and other organisations. For details telephone Summersdale Publishers on (+44-1243-771107), fax (+44-1243-786300) or email (nicky@summersdale.com).

CONTENTS

EDITOR'S NOTE

Sean O'Casey once said of his countrymen that 'they treat a joke as a serious thing, and a serious thing as a joke'. Hardly surprising, then, that Irish wit and logic is renowned the world over.

From George Bernard Shaw to Brendan Behan, the Emerald Isle boasts an abundance of wit-smiths: within these pages alone you'll find more laughs than you can shake a shamrock at.

Oscar Wilde once quite rightly pointed out that, 'Life is much too important a thing ever to talk seriously about it'; as the mirthful musings in this book show, the same rule applies to eating and drinking, love and marriage, work and money, and so much more...

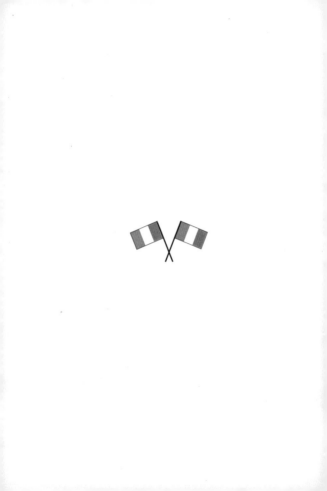

SHAMBHALA PUBLICATIONS, INC.

Mailing List
P.O. Box 308, Back Bay Annex
Boston, Massachusetts
02117

If you wish to receive a copy of the latest Shambhala Publications catalogue of books and to be placed on our mailing list, please send us this card, or e-mail us at: info@shambhala.com

PLEASE PRINT

Book in which this card was found

_____

NAME

_____

ADDRESS

_____

CITY & STATE

_____

ZIP OR POSTAL CODE   COUNTRY
                                      (if outside U.S.A.)

_____

E-MAIL ADDRESS

_____

INSULTS

In the human race, you came last.

SPIKE MILLIGAN

I loved her so much I named my
first ulcer after her.

DUSTY YOUNG

If you had a brain cell it would
die of loneliness.

JOHN O'DWYER

She has an ego like a raging tooth.

W. B. YEATS

He'd be out of his depth on
a wet pavement.

JOE O'SHEA

No, that skirt doesn't make you look fatter. How could it?

MAUREEN POTTER

Simon Cowell's waxwork in Madame Tussauds is more real than he is.

LOUIS WALSH

Your features don't seem to know
the value of teamwork.

GENE FITZPATRICK

The only thing my husband
ever achieved on his own was
his moustache.

JANE O'REILLY

Why don't you write books people can read?

NORA JOYCE TO HER HUSBAND JAMES

If I say that he's extremely stupid, I don't mean that in any derogatory sense.

BRENDAN O'CARROLL

For a young girl to be named 'wholesome' is perhaps the deadliest insult of all.

CAITLIN THOMAS

IRELAND AND THE IRISH

An Irishman was once asked to define winter. 'It's the time of year,' he explained, 'when it gets late early.'

TOM MCINTYRE

Irish women like the simple things
in life – like Irish men.

MARY COUGHLAN

Never hit an Irishman when he's
down. He might get up again.

SEAMUS O'LEARY

Dublin University contains the cream of Ireland – rich and thick.

SAMUEL BECKETT

The Irish, and I'm also guilty of this, think they invented everything.

BONO

Being Irish, he had an abiding sense of tragedy, which sustained him through temporary periods of joy.

WILLIAM BUTLER YEATS

A secret in Dublin means just telling one person at a time.

CIARÁN MACGONIGAL

I'm Irish. We
think sideways.

SPIKE MILLIGAN

The Irish love to be loved,
except by each other.

DAVID KENNY

The inner city architecture
of Dublin is like a lady in the
morning without her make-up on.

JIM TUNNEY

When anyone asks me
about the Irish character, I
say look at the trees. Maimed,
stark and misshapen, but
ferociously tenacious.

EDNA O'BRIEN

It's not that the Irish are cynical.
It's simply that they have a
wonderful lack of respect for
everything and everybody.

BRENDAN BEHAN

That's the Irish people all over
– they treat a joke as a serious
thing, and a serious thing
as a joke.

SEAN O'CASEY

An Irishman was asked if the Irish
always answered one question
with another. 'Who told you
that?' he replied.

NIALL TOIBIN

EATING
AND
DRINKING

How do you cross
Dublin without passing
a pub? Go into all
of them!

JAMES JOYCE, *ULYSSES*

Never eat on an empty stomach.

JASON BYRNE

Drink is your enemy.
Love your enemies.

SIL FOX

It was a bold man who ate
the first oyster.

JONATHAN SWIFT

A hot dog feeds the hand
that bites it.

DEREK DAVIS

The only reason I went
to America was because
I saw a sign saying
'Drink Canada Dry'.

GEORGE BEST

I lost so many years through drink, it was 1972 before I learned JFK had been assassinated.

DAVID KELLY

A restaurant I used to frequent in Cork advertised: 'Eat here and you'll never eat anywhere else again.'

NIALL TOIBIN

In England I'm regarded as an alcoholic. In Ireland they see me as a sissy drinker.

SHANE MACGOWAN

I finally found a diet that works in Ireland. I only eat when the weather's good.

HAL ROACH

Only in Ireland is the pint of stout
regarded as a digestif.

TERRY WOGAN

In 1969 I gave up drinking and sex.
It was the worst 20 minutes
of my life.

GEORGE BEST

I didn't fight my way to the top of the food chain to be a vegetarian.

JOE O'HERLIHY

Abstinence should always be practised in moderation.

JOE LYNCH

LOVE AND MARRIAGE

A man who says his wife can't take a joke forgets that she took him.

OSCAR WILDE

Foreplay, in Ireland, is the
technical term for taking
your shoes off.

JOSEPH O'CONNOR

I wonder what fool it was that
first invented kissing?

JONATHAN SWIFT

Love may make the
world go round, but not
as fast as whiskey.

RICHARD HARRIS

Marriage is forever – like cement.

PETER O'TOOLE

Safe sex to a Dubliner is doing it
when your wife's gone to bingo.

DAVID KENNY

We had a quiet wedding.
Her father had a silencer
on the shotgun.

SEAN KILROY

Give women the vote and in
five years' time there will be a
crushing tax on bachelors.

GEORGE BERNARD SHAW

I think, therefore I'm single.

SINEAD FLYNN

If there were no
husbands, who
would look after
our mistresses?

GEORGE MOORE

I'm hoarse listening to my
wife complaining.

BRENDAN BEHAN

Never make a task a pleasure,
as the man said when he dug his
wife's grave only three feet deep.

SEAMUS MCMANUS

I don't tell my wife anything. I figure that what she doesn't know won't hurt me.

DANNY CUMMINS

I'm giving up marriage for Lent.

BRIAN BEHAN

WORK AND MONEY

Work is the curse of the drinking classes.

OSCAR WILDE

My father is so long on the dole
he thinks a P45 is a gun.

BIG O

I have never liked working. To me
a job is an invasion of privacy.

DANNY MCGOORTY

The only thing that has to be
finished by next Friday is
next Thursday.

MAUREEN POTTER

Money couldn't buy friends, but
you get a better class of enemy.

SPIKE MILLIGAN

A man's respect for law and order exists in precise relationship to the size of his pay cheque.

ADAM CLAYTON

If anyone broke into our house, they'd leave a donation.

FRANK CARSON

Nothing is more
expensive than a girl
who's free for the
evening.

HAL ROACH

THE
ENGLISH
AND OTHER
FOREIGNERS

The English character is fearful of intellectuals in a way that Dracula had a thing about crosses.

DECLAN LYNCH

The British beatitudes are beer, business, bibles, bulldogs, battleships, buggery and bishops.

JAMES JOYCE

The Irish remember too much and the English too little.

EILIS O'HANLON

For many years I thought an innuendo was an Italian suppository.

SPIKE MILLIGAN

Americans will go on adoring me until I say something nice about them.

GEORGE BERNARD SHAW

We have really everything in common with America nowadays except, of course, language.

OSCAR WILDE, *THE CANTERVILLE GHOST*

De Valera is the greatest Irishman born in New York to a Spanish father who ever lived.

PAT FITZPATRICK

A Mexican straight flush is any five cards and a gun.

HUGH LEONARD

SPORT

Old golfers don't die.
They just putter out.

SIL FOX

Chelsea has just launched a new aftershave called 'The Special One' by U Go Boss.

PAT FLANAGAN ON JOSÉ MOURINHO'S DEPARTURE FROM THE FOOTBALL CLUB IN 2007

A golf club is a stick with a head on one end and a fool on the other.

DAMIEN MULDOON

My idea of exercise is striking a
match for a cigarette.

ANNE-MARIE SCANLON

It's always nice to start off with
a good result.

ROBBIE KEANE

I gave up shadow-boxing the night my shadow beat me up.

JAMES MCKEON

Peter Clohessy's main problem was that he couldn't stop jumping on hookers.

DERMOT MORGAN

Show me a dressing room of nice polite players and I'll show you a dressing room full of losers.

TONY CASCARINO

RELIGION

St Patrick brought
Christianity to Ireland.
It's a pity the idea never
caught on.

GEORGE BERNARD SHAW

Irish atheists have started a 'Dial-A-Prayer' service. When they phone, nobody answers.

HAL ROACH

I'm terrified about the day that I enter the gates of heaven and God says to me, 'Just a minute.'

MAUREEN O'HARA

Ireland remains a deeply
divided country, the two main
denominations being 'us'
and 'them'.

FRANK MCNALLY

When did I realise I was God?
Well, I was praying and I suddenly
realised I was talking to myself.

PETER O'TOOLE

I'm an Irish Catholic and I have a long iceberg of guilt.

EDNA O'BRIEN

When the gods want to punish us, they answer our prayers.

OSCAR WILDE

I'm an atheist... thank God.

DAVE ALLEN

Every saint has a past and
every sinner a future.

CALLUM BEST

I'm a bad Catholic. It's the religion
of all great artists.

BRENDAN BEHAN

LIFE

I'm not so sure if I believe in reincarnation. I can't even remember the things I've done in this life.

RICHARD HARRIS

Every dog has its day, but only a dog with a broken tail has a weak end.

SEAMUS O'LEARY

Life is a long preparation for something that never happens.

WILLIAM BUTLER YEATS

What do I know of man's destiny? I could tell you more about radishes.

SAMUEL BECKETT

Life is much too
important a thing ever
to talk seriously
about it.

OSCAR WILDE

I would like to divide my life into alternating periods of penance, cavorting and work.

EDNA O'BRIEN

We're not the men our fathers were. If we were we would be terribly old.

FLANN O'BRIEN

Every man desires to live long, but
no man wishes to be old.

JONATHAN SWIFT

Glory is fleeting, but obscurity
is forever.

THOMAS MOORE

All I want to do is sit on my arse,
fart and think of Dante.

SAMUEL BECKETT

The day after tomorrow is the
third day of the rest of your life.

GEORGE CARLIN

THE BIG
SLEEP

I intend to die in bed at 110 writing poetry, sipping Guinness and serenading a woman.

RICHARD HARRIS

I'm not afraid of dying – I just don't want to be there when it happens.

SPIKE MILLIGAN

If my father was alive to see the modern world, he'd turn in his grave.

MICHAEL O'DOHERTY

I watched a funeral go by and asked who was dead. A man said, 'The fella in the box.'

DAVE ALLEN

I am told he makes a very handsome corpse, and becomes his coffin prodigiously.

OLIVER GOLDSMITH

An undertaker is
the last man to let
you down.

JIMMY O'DEA

There's no point taking out life insurance. My uncle did and he died all the same.

SEAN KILROY

A doctor's reputation is made by the number of eminent men who die under his care.

GEORGE BERNARD SHAW

My grandmother made dying
her life's work.

HUGH LEONARD

Either that wallpaper goes, or I do.

OSCAR WILDE'S LAST WORDS

I told you I was ill.

SPIKE MILLIGAN'S EPITAPH

Funerals in Ireland are so jolly,
they should be called funferalls.

JAMES JOYCE

POLITICS

The weak are a long time in politics.

NEIL SHAND

If the word 'No' was removed from the English language, Ian Paisley would be speechless.

JOHN HUME

He knows nothing and thinks he knows everything. That clearly points to a career in politics.

GEORGE BERNARD SHAW

Don't vote. The government
always gets in.

FRANK KELLY

Making peace, I have found, is
much harder than making war.

GERRY ADAMS

Arnold Schwarzenegger is the
governor of California. He got
there by lifting things.

DYLAN MORAN

Ireland has the best politicians
money can buy.

SAM SNORT

My electioneering style? I kiss the mothers and shake hands with the babies.

JOE COSTELLO

A man should always be
drunk when he talks of politics.
It's the only way to make
them important.

SEAN O'CASEY

Why do you stand for election
to get a seat?

DONAL FOLEY

The Greeks came up with
democracy, but they had no
intention of everyone having it.

BONO

If Irish politicians were laid end to
end, they'd have their feet in
each other's mouths.

SEAMUS O'LEARY

THE ARTS

Sleep is an excellent
way of listening to
an opera.

JAMES STEPHENS

Writing is like getting married.
One should never commit oneself
until one is amazed at one's luck.

IRIS MURDOCH

Never judge a book by its movie.

CYRIL CUSACK

Memoirs are a well-known
form of fiction.

FRANK HARRIS

If there's music in hell,
it'll be bagpipes.

JOE TOMELTY

A poet can survive anything
but a misprint.

OSCAR WILDE

Murder is considered less immoral
than fornication in literature.

GEORGE MOORE

I write like a
snail trailing slime.
But sometimes the
slime glistens.

JOHN BANVILLE

If you're interested in finding out
more about our humour books, follow us
on Twitter: @SummersdaleLOL

www.summersdale.com